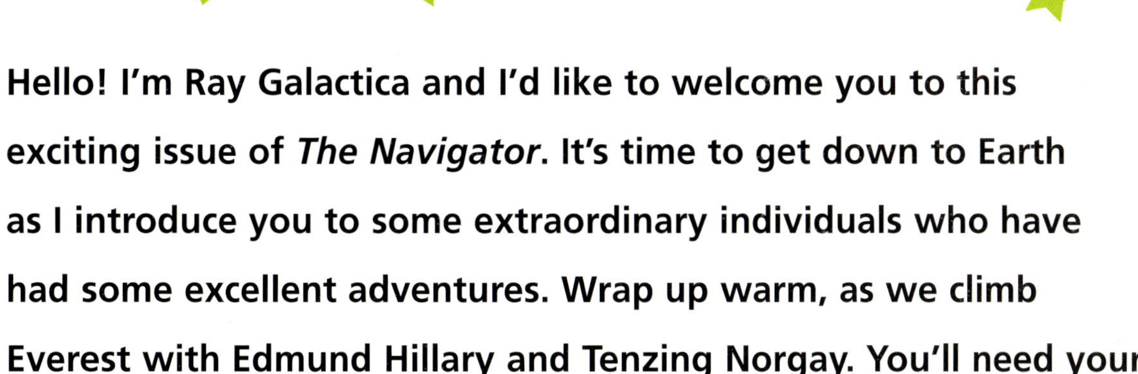

Hello! I'm Ray Galactica and I'd like to welcome you to this exciting issue of *The Navigator*. It's time to get down to Earth as I introduce you to some extraordinary individuals who have had some excellent adventures. Wrap up warm, as we climb Everest with Edmund Hillary and Tenzing Norgay. You'll need your walking boots too, as we boldly go into uncharted territory with two American explorers. You'll also have the chance to get in the saddle and find out about a scooter millionaire and a giant wooden horse.

Onwards, my friends!

Text Type	Literacy Skills	Wider Curriculum Links
Newspaper: Recount	Language analysis; distinguishing between fact and opinion; close reading	**History** Units 14 and 15: Who were the Ancient Greeks? How do we use Ancient Greek ideas today?
Persuasive/ Report	Language analysis; expressing and justifying opinions	**History** Unit 11: What was it like for children living in Victorian Britain?
Recount	Inferential comprehension; expressing and justifying opinions; language analysis; asking questions	**Geography** Unit 15: The mountain environment
Report	Summarising information	**Geography** Unit 14: Investigating rivers
Recount	Summarising content; expressing and justifying opinions; authorial intent	**Geography** Unit 14: Investigating rivers
Recount	Inferential comprehension; asking questions	**Science** Unit 6B: Micro-organisms
Recount	Information retrieval; asking questions	**Design and Technology** Unit 6D: Controllable vehicles
Report	Summarising information; language analysis; authorial intent	
Report	Summarising information	
Report	Interpreting information; close reading; language analysis	**PSHE:** Preparing to play an active role as citizens
Fun Spread		
		ICT: Year 6 Schemes of Work

Troy falls after Greek horseplay

The wooden horse inside the city walls

Gift horse proves deadly ploy

The Greeks pulled off a spectacular stunt last night when a wooden horse carrying Greek soldiers was pulled inside the city gates of Troy in Asia Minor.

The giant horse was earlier left on the seashore by the Greeks, who went into retreat yesterday, ending their ten-year siege of the city. Initial reports suggested it was a peace offering to the goddess Athene. The horse was taken inside the city gates on the orders of the Trojan King Priam. Witnesses say it was after dark when the horse unloaded its deadly cargo of Greek soldiers who opened the city gates.

The wooden horse

The face that launched a thousand ships

Troy has been under siege since the King of Sparta's wife Helen, voted 'most beautiful woman in the world', ran off with the Trojan diplomat, Paris. Many experts believed the city's defences could not be broken. In the end, it was a cunning trick master-minded by the Greek hero Odysseus that led to the fall of Troy. Trojans had been celebrating the end of the war last night after Greek camps were seen burning. It now appears the Greeks had anchored off nearby Tenedos, waiting for a signal from the crack team of soldiers inside the horse inside the city.

One of Odysseus' men said last night,

"The guys did well. It wasn't easy, being cooped up inside that thing. We didn't know whether the Trojans were on to us or not. We had to stay absolutely still and quiet, even when the horse was being dragged inside the city walls. The worst bit was hearing the Trojans say they should chuck the horse over the city walls, or set fire to it. Some of us began to sweat then, I can tell you! Then this spear crashed into the side of the horse and we thought the game was up."

The Trojan Priest Laocoon, who threw the spear at the horse, was one of many who warned against bringing it inside the city. One Trojan, who escaped the fighting that followed, said the horse should have been destroyed on the beach.

"It was madness. They should have broken it open where it was. There were rumours flying around that it was some sort of trick. It was so big, they had a job getting it inside the city walls. There were women throwing roses at it, like it was some kind of gift. Everyone went mad last night. That was when it happened. We were sitting ducks."

Hundreds of Trojan men and boys have been killed in the fighting and women and girls taken into slavery. But reports say Helen escaped with her life, and is being taken back to Sparta.

Map of the area

Education for girls

Girls at school in 1860

Girls, do you think that going to school is a waste of time? If so, you are living in the wrong age! If you had lived 150 years ago, you would have found that almost everyone agreed with you. Most people thought that only boys should be taught academic subjects. However, a few women passionately believed that girls should be educated too.

Miss Buss and Miss Beale

Frances Buss and Dorothea Beale were two pioneers of secondary education for girls. In 1854, Miss Beale established Cheltenham Ladies' College as the first school to teach girls academic subjects. Miss Buss founded North London Collegiate School and Camden School for Girls, with low fees and high academic standards.

At the time, some people made fun of Miss Buss and Miss Beale. This rhyme was published in a newspaper:

Miss Buss and Miss Beale
Cupid's darts do not feel.
How different from us,
Miss Beale and Miss Buss.

The Victorians wrote pamphlets to inform and persuade people about different subjects. The pamphlet opposite is like those written in the 1860s to argue in favour of education for girls.

E·D·U·C·A·T·I·O·N· F·O·R· G·I·R·L·S

Education helps the individual and it helps the nation, SO WHY IS IT DENIED TO GIRLS?

Until 1844, children worked in the most abominable situations for up to eighteen hours a day. Those who worked down the mines never saw daylight. We have made GREAT ADVANCES since then. Today, children cannot work more than ten hours a day and many go to school. Most children can now read and write. BUT WE MUST NOT STOP HERE.

Schools teach girls to sew and to clean, but what does this qualify them to do? To work as domestic maids, in the service of wealthy households. And why do these girls prefer to take jobs at lower wages in factories, rather than work in domestic service? The answer is that domestic servants, who work incessantly all hours of the day, are LITTLE BETTER THAN SLAVES. Let us teach girls academic subjects so that they can better themselves by earning good money in offices. An educated girl can keep accounts and write letters as well as any male clerk.

More and more boys continue their schooling beyond thirteen years of age. They learn Mathematics, Science, Latin, Greek and History. Many go on to university to become theologians, doctors, politicians, or to take up other positions of power. WHY CANNOT GIRLS DO THIS TOO?

IS MARRIAGE THE ONLY OPTION for young ladies? Are intelligent, energetic young women fit only to be the dutiful wives of powerful men, and the doting mothers of sons who will form the next generation of powerful men? Men say that women are too weak and frail to understand politics, that they are not capable of voting intelligently. Let us educate these women and then we shall see what they are capable of achieving!

Britain is the wealthiest and most powerful nation in the world. It needs an educated workforce, but, most of all, BRITAIN NEEDS EDUCATED WOMEN.

Mountain mystery

Every encyclopaedia will tell you that Edmund Hillary and Tenzing Norgay were the first people to climb Mount Everest, the highest mountain in the world. They crossed moving ice-fields and survived blizzards as cold as those in the Arctic to reach the top of the mountain in 1953. But were they really the first people to stand on the summit?

Many climbers have attempted to reach the summit of Mount Everest

George Mallory and his team of climbers

George Mallory's expeditions

In the 1920s, George Mallory led three expeditions to Mount Everest. The climbers were helped by Sherpas – local men who were used to the steep mountains and freezing climate, and who helped to carry their supplies. The air near the summit is so thin, however, that even the Sherpas could scarcely breathe and every movement was a great effort. The party had bottles of oxygen, which the Sherpas called 'English air', to help them breathe. But the breathing equipment was unreliable, and the bottles of gas were very heavy.

The third attempt

In 1924, after he had twice failed to reach the summit of Everest, Mallory asked a man called Andrew Irvine to join him for a third expedition. Irvine was not a climber, but an engineer who was good at repairing the oxygen masks. The climbers set up a series of camps on their way up the mountain, with the final camp less than 1219 metres below the summit. On 8 June, Mallory and Irvine set out for the top. They were last seen climbing upwards, just 244 metres below the summit, when they disappeared into cloud.

Mallory and Irvine never returned. No one knows what happened to them or whether they reached the top. There is one piece of evidence which might reveal what happened – Mallory's camera. If they had reached the summit, the film would include a photo of their triumph. Could it be located?

The unanswered question

Mallory's body was found in 1999

Since Hillary and Norgay's success in 1953, many teams of climbers have reached the summit. In 1975, a Chinese climber reported that he had seen a body dressed in 1920s clothing less than 914 metres from the summit. It could only have been Mallory or Irvine. In 1999, a new expedition set out for Everest to search for Mallory, Irvine and the all-important camera. The expedition followed the Chinese climber's directions and found a body, dressed in woollen jerseys, leather boots and climbing jacket. These clothes were in sharp contrast to their own hi-tech, wind-proof suits. The body was Mallory's. His right leg was broken and his skull was cracked, which suggested that he had fallen down a steep slope. But his camera was not with him. Had he dropped it or given it to Irvine? In spite of further searching, neither Irvine nor the camera has been found, and the mystery remains unsolved.

Mount Everest is named after George Everest, the surveyor who measured its height in 1856 and declared it the highest mountain in the world. But the mountain already had a name. The local people call it Chomolungma, which means 'Goddess Mother of the World'.

Mount Everest fact file

Position: In the Himalayan mountains, between Nepal and Tibet
Height: 8840 metres
Temperature: Can drop as low as −43° C

The great continent

The continent of North America is a vast, rugged land with thick forests, mighty rivers and snow-covered mountains. Until as recently as 200 years ago, this land was largely unexplored. Native Americans were thinly scattered across the whole continent, while the people who had come from Europe had settled mostly along the eastern side, on land between the Atlantic coast and the broad Mississippi River.

Areas settled in America by 1800

The search for new land

The Mississippi formed a natural frontier between the settled and the unexplored land, but traders and fur-trappers had travelled far beyond it. They had spoken with Native Americans, who told them about the rolling prairies, high mountains and great forests that lay 'way out west'.

The United States president, Thomas Jefferson, was keen for someone to explore these lands. He wanted to claim them for the United States and open up new routes for trade. The American government agreed to provide $2500 to fund an expedition.

CROSSING A CONTINENT

Lewis and Clark

President Jefferson chose his private secretary to lead the expedition. Meriwether Lewis was a captain who had served in the army. Lewis invited his friend William Clark to share the leadership with him.

The two men had spent much time along the frontier and had had friendly contact with Native Americans. They hoped to learn a lot from the expedition – about the land itself, the people who lived on it, and the many species of animals and plants.

The natural landscape of America

Meriwether Lewis   *William Clark*

Making plans

The best way of travelling though uncharted land is by water. Lewis and Clark hoped to find a water route that would carry them across North America to the Pacific Ocean. They planned to start from St Louis, a town on the Mississippi River. From there, they would sail north-west up the Missouri River, which they hoped would eventually lead them to the Pacific Ocean.

During the winter of 1803–04, the two men planned the trip. They ordered their supplies and gathered together a group of soldiers, hunters, trappers, boatmen and servants to accompany them on the expedition. On a bright spring morning in May 1804, Lewis and Clark set out.

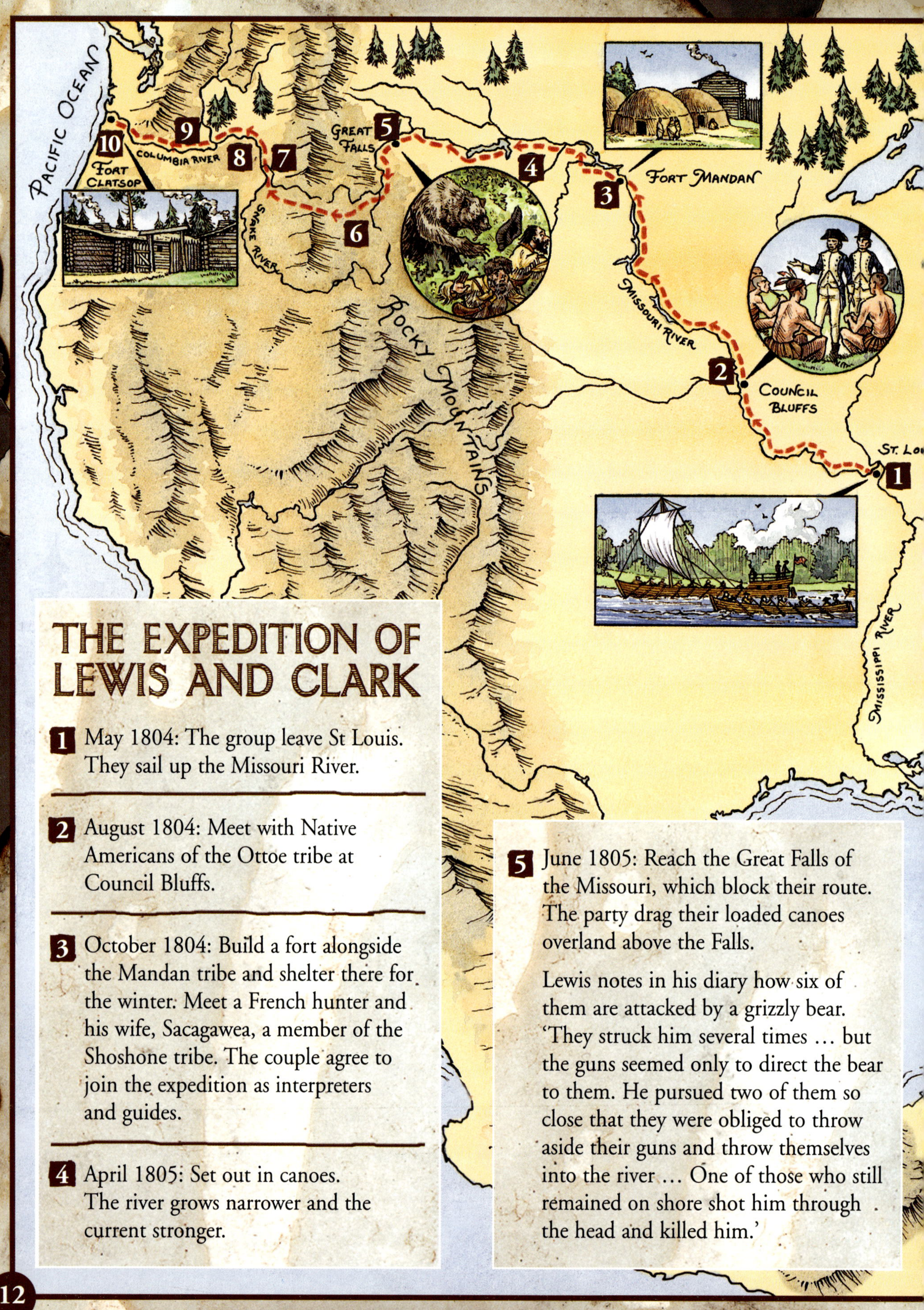

THE EXPEDITION OF LEWIS AND CLARK

1 May 1804: The group leave St Louis. They sail up the Missouri River.

2 August 1804: Meet with Native Americans of the Ottoe tribe at Council Bluffs.

3 October 1804: Build a fort alongside the Mandan tribe and shelter there for the winter. Meet a French hunter and his wife, Sacagawea, a member of the Shoshone tribe. The couple agree to join the expedition as interpreters and guides.

4 April 1805: Set out in canoes. The river grows narrower and the current stronger.

5 June 1805: Reach the Great Falls of the Missouri, which block their route. The party drag their loaded canoes overland above the Falls.

Lewis notes in his diary how six of them are attacked by a grizzly bear. 'They struck him several times … but the guns seemed only to direct the bear to them. He pursued two of them so close that they were obliged to throw aside their guns and throw themselves into the river … One of those who still remained on shore shot him through the head and killed him.'

6 July 1805: Reach the Rocky Mountains and have to abandon their canoes. They now pass through the lands of the Shoshone tribe, whose chief is Sacagawea's brother. Shoshone guides help them across the mountains – the hardest part of the trip.

7 August 1805: With the Rockies behind them, they continue on water.

8 October 1805: Travel along the Snake River to the great Columbia River. The land is more forested now, and the weather is foggy and wet.

9 November 1805: After over 18 months, the group gets its first glimpse of the Pacific. Clark writes in his journal, 'Great joy in camp, the ocean is in view.'

10 10 December 1805: The travellers reach the Pacific shore and build Fort Clatsop in which to shelter for the winter.

Back home

Lewis and Clark returned to St Louis in September 1806. They had been gone two years, four months and nine days, and had travelled about 9 650 kilometres. Although they did not find an easy water route to the Pacific, the expedition was a great success. The two men's report about the country, the Native Americans, and the animals and plants gave the US government an accurate picture of the continent. There were vast areas of fertile land, rich in timber, beaver and salmon. This encouraged settlers and traders to push out west and extend their country's borders. But this success came at a price – the old way of life of the Native Americans was about to disappear for good.

A foot and mouth diary

For farmers, spring is traditionally the season of new life. However, in February 2001, all that changed due to an outbreak of the highly infectious foot and mouth disease. Many British farmers were devastated when their cattle, sheep and pigs had to be slaughtered to prevent the disease from spreading across the whole country. Only cloven-footed animals become infected with the disease. The first signs are blisters around the mouth, or sore feet.

In Michael Morpurgo's book *Out of the Ashes*, Rebecca Morley, a thirteen-year-old farmer's daughter, records her thoughts and feelings about the foot and mouth crisis in her diary. When she writes the following diary entry, she is staying at her aunt's house, unable to return to her parents' farm due to restrictions on the movement of people and animals in infected areas.

A sheep being checked by a vet

Signs outside an infected farm

A farm infected with foot and mouth

12 Monday

I can't put into words what I feel. There are no words black enough to say what I've got to say.

We were having supper when the phone rang. Auntie Liz answered it. I knew right away something was wrong, and I knew from the moment she looked at me exactly what it was. She handed me the phone. Mum was trying not to cry as she told me. She hadn't wanted to worry me about it yesterday, she said, but the vet had been called in yesterday morning. Dad had found blisters on the feet of one of our sows, Jessica, and was worried about a couple of sheep that were limping badly. Tests had confirmed it. We had foot and mouth disease on the farm. There was an 'A' notice on the farm gate which meant no one was allowed in or out except the vets and the slaughterers. The animals would be put down tomorrow. So I'd have to stay with Auntie Liz until it was all over. It would be the best place for me, she said.

When I asked how Dad was, she said he was very calm, as if he'd been expecting it all along. She said she'd phone again tomorrow, and that she loved me. I don't remember the last time she said that to me. She sounded almost like a different person.

I've been sitting here on the bed in a daze ever since. Not crying. I can't cry. It's me who's done this, it must be. I brought the infection back with me from Mr Bailey's farm. Ruby or Bobs or me, but whichever of us it was, it had been my doing, my fault. I had sentenced our animals to death.

Throughout 2001, nearly four million animals from almost a thousand farms were slaughtered as a result of the foot and mouth crisis.

Dominic McVey

London-based Dominic McVey is an inspiration to all would-be entrepreneurs – especially very young ones. For Dominic was just thirteen, and still at school, when he set himself up in business. Three years later he was a millionaire.

Scooter Millionaire

Of course, you don't automatically get rich when you start a business, whatever age you are. Success like that depends on many things, including energy, personal resources, and luck. Luck can play the most important part of all. Dominic was lucky. But he also had the idea that hit the spot with a lot of people at just the right time – distributing VIZA scooters. "I went into scooters because I like them and thought they would catch on. They're a great solution to commuting through traffic in London," says Dominic.

Dominic with a VIZA scooter

Dominic didn't invent or design these scooters, but he had the imagination to see that they could catch on in a big way. He started importing them from the United States, and now, thanks to him all sorts of people now scoot around European towns and cities on them: business people, shop assistants, hairdressers, butchers, florists – as well as teenagers and children, of course.

The scooters have been very popular

Dominic was interested in making money from a very early age. He used to read the *Financial Times* while his friends were playing computer games and watching TV. Before setting up the scooter distribution business he used his dad's credit card (with Dad's knowledge) to buy stocks and shares.

These days, Dominic employs people to handle most aspects of the business for him. Now that he's made his fortune, is he going to keep on distributing scooters? "The scooters are cool," Dominic says, "but I'd like to move into other areas. I want to be Dominic McVey, businessman. I'm not going to tie myself down to one thing." Dominic's company, Scooters UK Ltd, is said to be worth £5m, with his personal wealth estimated at around £1.5m.

The one and only you!

Has anyone ever told you that you're unique? They're right! You *are* unique. In this world of more than six billion people, there is no one exactly like you. There are people with the same colour hair, the same colour eyes, and even the same shaped nose as you. But even if you had an identical twin, there would still be many differences between the two of you.

What makes you unique?

It's all down to DNA. DeoxyriboNucleic Acid is a chemical substance found in every cell in every part of your body. DNA looks like a long twisted 'ladder' which contains genes which are responsible for every detail of your appearance. In other words, the genes in your DNA make you who you are – they determine the colour of your hair and eyes, the shape of your face, and even your fingerprints!

Family ties

Your physical features come from the genes that you receive from your parents. But what happens if one parent is very tall and the other is really short? You can't be tall and short at the same time can you? What if your mum has black hair and your dad has blond hair? Will that mean that half of your hair is blond and the other half is black? No, it won't!

Designer genes

Your features are given to you by your parents in a mix-and-match pattern. For each particular feature, for example eye colour, you get one gene from your father and one gene from your mother. Some genes are called dominant. The dominant genes have more power than other genes (known as recessive genes) so they control what gets handed down to you. For example, if you receive a gene for brown eyes from your mother and one for blue eyes from your father, then your eyes will probably be brown because the gene for brown eyes is dominant – in other words, it is stronger than the recessive gene for blue eyes.

Hair-raising stuff!

The gene for a 'widows peak' is also dominant.

A widow's peak is a V-shaped growth of hair towards the centre of the hairline. The child of a mother with a straight hairline and a father with a widow's peak shaped hairline will have a widow's peak hairline like their father.

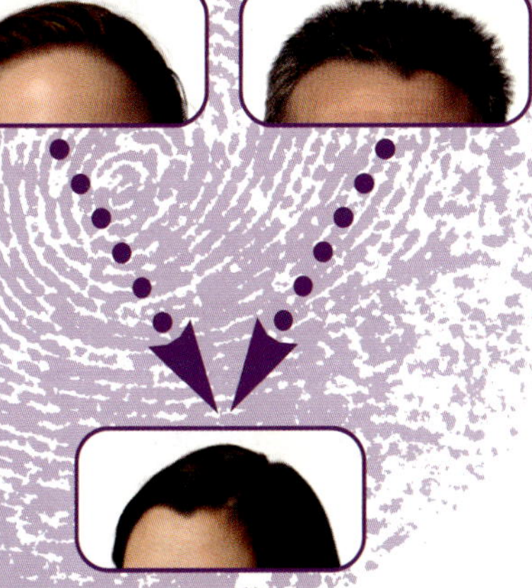

Tongue twisters!

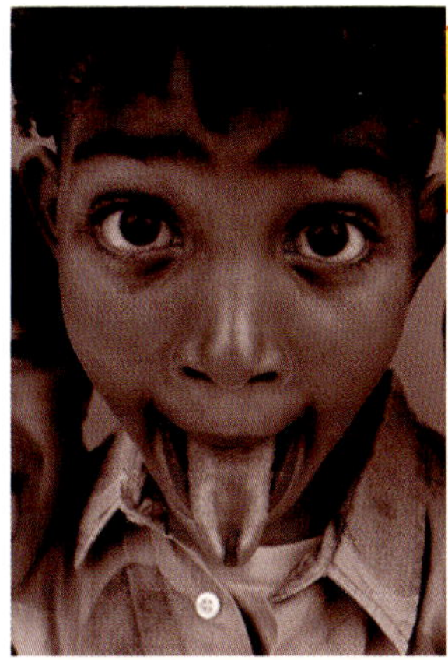

The gene for tongue-rolling is dominant too. If one of your parents can roll their tongue, then you will be able to roll yours. If you have brothers and sisters, they should be able to roll their tongues too. Why not give it a go!

Inky fingers

You are unique! The proof is right at your fingertips! No one, not even identical twins, have the same fingerprints. Those tiny ridges on the tips of your fingers were formed before you were born.

Catching criminals

If you ever watch television programmes about the police, you will already know that fingerprints can help a detective to track down a criminal. Fingerprinting has been used to identify people for more than a hundred years. It was in the 1880s that scientists realised that no two people's fingerprints are the same. Then fingerprinting became an important part of police investigations. It could be used as part of the evidence in court to prove a suspect committed a crime. The first time this happened was in 1901.

This is still true today. At the scene of a crime, detectives look for fingerprints that a criminal may have left behind on objects that they touched. Though the fingerprints are not always visible to the naked eye, they show up after a special black powder has been brushed on them. This process is known as 'dusting for prints'. Once detectives find a suspect for the crime, they dip his or her fingertips in ink and make a record of the prints left behind when the fingertips are pressed onto paper.

Yours for life!

The pattern on your fingertips stays the same even as your hands get bigger and your body gets taller. When you are eighty years old, your fingertips will have the same design as they had on the day you were born. Even if you are wearing a disguise on the rest of your body, fingerprints can always reveal your true identity!

There are four kinds of fingerprints: arches, loops, whorls and composites (which are a mix of the first three!).

Dusting for prints

Has someone been rummaging in your room? If so, they will have left fingerprints on anything hard and shiny. Be a detective and dust for prints!

Here's how:

- Use a paintbrush to dust talcum powder lightly onto the object.

- Very gently, blow away most of the powder.

- If there is a greasy fingerprint there, some of the powder will stick.

- Use a magnifying glass to examine the fingerprint and check which pattern it has.

- Check the pattern against the fingerprints of your main suspects!

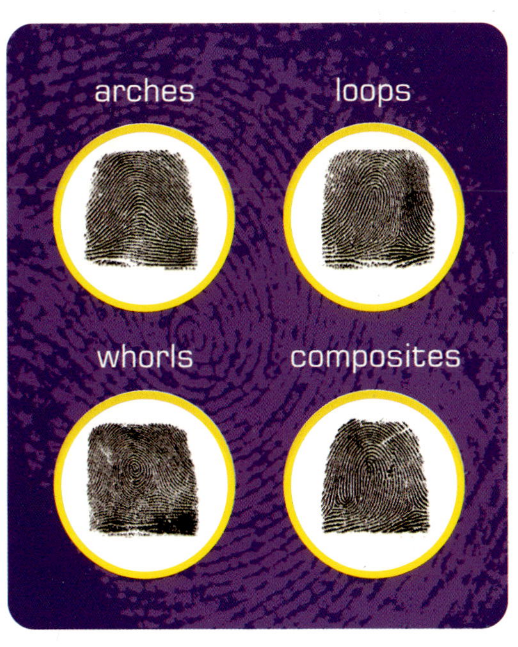

Children's

Most children in the West take their basic rights for granted. They don't go hungry. They have roofs over their heads. They receive full-time education. They aren't made to work for little or no money. But many children in other parts of the world aren't so lucky. So, human rights organisations and charities have been set up in many countries to try and help them.

The United Nations Convention on the Rights of the Child

The Convention on the Rights of the Child is the first international agreement to list essential human rights for children. The Convention's core demands are that all children should have the right to human dignity, to be protected from exploitation and abuse, and to be free to take part fully in family life and the cultural and social life of the community. The Convention has been agreed by almost 200 countries.

National Society for the Prevention of Cruelty to Children

There are a number of organisations whose prime function is to protect and help fund the well-being of underprivileged and mistreated children. One, the NSPCC, is the only national organisation in England, Wales and Northern Ireland devoted to eliminating child abuse. The NSPCC campaigns to improve the welfare and protection of children.

The NSPCC is '… *an organisation which will fight to obtain the citizenship of every child and justice for all children.*'

Benjamin Waugh, Founder of the NSPCC, 1884

The NSPCC exists to:
- Prevent children suffering harm as a result of ill-treatment.
- Help protect children at risk from such harm.
- Help abused children to overcome the effects of such harm.
- Work to protect children from further harm.

Rights

Sweatshops

The term 'sweatshop' was first coined in 19th century America to describe a place where people worked for very little money making clothes. In the 21st century there are still a great many sweatshops in various parts of the world. Often the workers are children.

'Students Against Sweatshops', started by students at a handful of American colleges and universities, has spread right across North America. Students have organised sweatshop fashion shows and other protests to demand that their places of education do not sell clothes or other things made by children in sweatshops.

Is our government doing enough for children?

A United Nations committee criticised the previous British government for not giving children a big enough say in issues that affect them. The committee also said more work was needed to tackle violence against children, and poverty and inequality.

The government claims that it is trying to avoid mistakes made in the past. It plans to overhaul the care system and reduce the risk of abuse. The government says it listens to children when formulating policy, and is 'improving services to children right across the board.'

Lateral thinking

Lateral thinking puzzles are about strange situations which need explanations. The term 'lateral thinking' was invented in 1967 by a Maltese doctor called Edward de Bono. It means solving a problem by looking at the situation from a new angle. De Bono believes that in a world that is always changing, people need to find new and creative solutions to difficult problems. Lateral thinking is not only for businessmen and scientists. You can do it too!

Have a go at the following puzzles. When you think you know the solutions, check your answers against the correct ones printed upside down at the bottom of the page. Remember, things aren't always what they seem!

1 It's a knockout

A man walked into a bar, and before he could say a word, was knocked unconscious. Why?

2 Wet weather

Four friends were walking back from work when it started to rain. Three of them got wet hair, but one of them didn't, even though he was not wearing a hat or carrying an umbrella. How could this be?

3 Carrot conundrum

Five pieces of coal, a carrot and a scarf were lying on the lawn. Nobody put them on the lawn. How did they get there?

4 Rider's riddle

A man rode into town on Friday. He stayed for three nights and then left on Friday. How was this possible?

5 Last legs

Hiding under a table at his sister's birthday party, Ben could see eight pairs of legs walking around in the room. After a while, he watched everyone go into the kitchen for some food. There were still six legs in the living room. How could this be?

Byte-Sized ICT

Troy falls after Greek horseplay

Old news

Can you imagine how modern newspapers would have reported some events in history? What would they have said about King Henry VIII getting married for the sixth time? Or about Britain being invaded by the Romans or Vikings? Which stories would have made the front page?

Have a go at writing a newspaper report about another event in history. Think about whether the report would show bias towards a particular viewpoint. How will you hint that you support one side or the other? Don't forget to include a catchy headline and a few quotes from experts or eyewitnesses, to add interest to your story.

You could use a publishing program to present your report. This will give you a newspaper-style layout with columns, and spaces for pictures and headlines. Try to think of a suitable name for your newspaper. Make sure you type the name in large bold letters.

Education for girls

Victorian education research challenge

Try using the Internet or a CD-ROM to find out five facts about education during Victorian times.

If you use the Internet, you will need to use a search engine to begin to find useful sites. Remember to think about typing in key words when requesting a search. If you type in 'Victorians' you will get far too many hits! Use the word 'and' to include two or more key words. If you find a good site, it may include some links to other useful sites. If you have watched a schools' television programme about the Victorians, you may find it has its own website. Look out for the web address (called a 'URL') at the end of the programme.

The one and only you!

Only me!

How well can you disguise yourself? Try taking some digital photos of yourself and some friends in disguise. You could wear hats, coats, false glasses and even wigs.

Print out the photographs and ask other members of your class (or another class) to guess who's who. If you think it is a bit tricky, try typing in the names of everyone and let people guess which name goes with which picture.

Along the Missouri

Atlas evaluation

Atlases on CD-ROM allow you to research the geography of different areas by viewing maps in different ways and zooming in and out. Have a go at finding out more about North America using an atlas on CD-ROM.

Evaluate the CD-ROM by thinking about how easy it was to use, how clearly linked the different screens were and how well the screens were arranged. What mark would you give it out of 10? If you have two atlases available, you could compare the two. Or why not compare a traditional book atlas with a CD-ROM version? Do they both have uses? What are the advantages and disadvantages of each?

Mountain mystery

Diary of a climber

What do you think happened to Mallory and Irvine on Everest? Do you think they reached the top? Using a word processor, try typing a diary as if you were Mallory. Imagine what would be going through your mind and what the conditions must have been like. Try to convey your feelings as well as reporting events.

When you have finished, save and print your work and then ask a friend to read it with you. Discuss if you think you could improve it in any way. Can you spot any mistakes, such as missing full stops or capital letters? Mark up your printout and then return to the computer to make any changes. (If you prefer, you could read and edit your work on screen.) Print out your edited version and compare the two printouts. Then show your teacher how you have proof-read, redrafted and edited your work.

Lateral thinking

Conundrum cartoons

Why not use an art package to illustrate one of the puzzles on pages 24 and 25? Try to show all the main items mentioned in the puzzle.

If you're feeling clever, you could even create a lateral thinking puzzle for your classmates to solve and produce an illustration for that. You will need to think about using words that could have two meanings.

Glossary

abominable	shocking or dreadful
academic	requiring you to read, study and think
accurate	correct or exact
blizzard	a fierce storm of wind and snow
cloven-footed	with hooves divided into two toes, like pigs, sheep, cows, goats and deer
diplomat	an official who represents his or her country abroad
domestic maids	servants who do the housework
eliminating	getting rid of, wiping out
entrepreneurs	people who start up new businesses, especially risky ones
fertile	where crops grow well
formulating	working something out and putting it in a clear way
frontier	the border between two countries, or the end of a settled region
horseplay	rough and tumble, messing around

interpreters	people who translate what someone is saying into another language
overhaul	to look something over carefully and make sure it works properly
pamphlets	booklets in paper covers
rugged	rough and uneven
sentenced	officially given a punishment
settled	where people had made their homes
slaughtered	killed
species	a group of animals, the members of which have similar characteristics
summit	the top, peak
theologians	people who study God and religion
trappers	people who lived in the forests, trapping animals for their fur
uncharted	never been mapped
unique	the only one of its kind
unreliable	not to be trusted

Index